We Celebrate
Hanukkah

Bobbie Kalman

Susan Hughes
Cecilia Ohm-Ericksen

The Holidays & Festivals Series

 Toronto New York Crabtree Publishing Company

The Holidays and Festivals Series
Created by Bobbie Kalman

Written by:
Susan Hughes

Illustrations:
Color illustrations by Cecilia Ohm-Ericksen
Pages 7, 10-11, 14, 18-19, 30-31, 38-39, by Chuck Ryder
Pages 22-23, 26-27, by Lisa Crouch
Pages 34-35, 47 by Bruce Archer
Pages 50-51, 54-55 by Maggi McConnell
© Crabtree Publishing Company

Editor-in-Chief:
Bobbie Kalman

Editors:
Rachel Atlas
Dan Liebman
Susan Hughes
Catherine Johnston

Art direction:
Susan Hughes
Catherine Johnston

Design and mechanicals:
Elaine Macpherson Enterprises Limited

For Judie

Cataloguing in Publication Data
Kalman, Bobbie, 1947-
    We celebrate Hanukkah

(The Holidays and festivals series)
Includes index.
ISBN 0-86505-045-7 (bound)
ISBN 0-86505-055-4 (pbk.)

1. Hanukkah - Juvenile literature. I. Hughes,
Susan, 1960- . II. Ohm-Ericksen, Cecilia.
III. Title. IV. Series.

BM695.H3K34 1986   j394.2'68296435

350 Fifth Ave., Suite 3308
New York, N.Y. 10118

360 York Road, R.R.4
Niagara-on-the-Lake, Ontario L0S 1J0

73 Lime Walk
Headington, Oxford OX3 7AD

Contents

5 Celebrate with us!

6 The origins of Hanukkah

8 Cleaning the Temple

10 When does Hanukkah come?

12 A celebration of peace

14 A joyful time

17 See them glow

18 Make a clay menorah

20 Festivals of light

22 What it means to me

25 Hanukkah words

26 Praying for peace

28 Foods for a feast

30 Special Hanukkah foods

32 Happy endings

34 Dreidel, dreidel, dreidel!

36 The secret of the dreidels

38 Oh, dreidel I will play!

40 Sharing at Hanukkah

42 Homemade Hanukkah gifts

44 A zany Hanukkah

46 Ways of celebrating

48 Preparing for a Hanukkah party!

50 Hanukkah games

53 Be My Shadow

54 The last night of Hanukkah

56 Index

4

Celebrate with us!

It's the twenty-fifth of Kislev.
Hanukkah is here,
Bringing eight days of happiness
To friends and family dear.

The candles in the menorah
We will light every night
In memory of the first Hanukkah oil
That burned so long and bright.

We will sing "Rock of Ages."
Can you sing along?
And after that, we might make up
A brand-new Hanukkah song.

Our parents will surprise us
With chocolate coins called gelt.
Then tasty latkes we'll enjoy.
I'll have to loosen my belt!

We'll all play with the dreidels
And watch them as they spin,
Just as the earth is turning.
I win, and then you win!

We'll hear the stories of Hanukkahs
Celebrated in the past,
Of the Maccabean struggles
And their victory at last.

The candles will start to flicker
And we will start to yawn.
The first night of Hanukkah
Will very soon be gone!

The origins of Hanukkah

Thousands of years ago, Jews lived in Judea. Judea was the southern part of Palestine which was on the east coast of the Mediterranean Sea. Israel and part of Jordan are now where Palestine used to be. As they do today, the Jews believed in a religion called Judaism.

The threats of King Antiochus

For hundreds of years, Judea was ruled by men who were not Jews. Most of the rulers allowed the Jews to follow their own laws and religion — until 175 B.C., when King Antiochus became the leader of Judea. He would not allow the Jews to follow their laws. He believed that everyone in Judea should practice the religion of the Greeks. Antiochus commanded all the Jews to give up their beliefs. He threatened to kill any Jew who did not follow his rules.

A small group gave up their faith, but many Jews refused to give up Judaism. They secretly continued to read the *Torah*. They secretly obeyed the Jewish laws, not the laws of Antiochus!

Mattathias sets an example

Mattathias lived with his five sons in a village called Modin. He was an important and respected Jewish priest. King Antiochus believed that if Mattathias gave up his faith, other Jews would follow his example. The King sent his soldiers to visit Mattathias. They offered him large amounts of money to turn his back on God, but Mattathias refused. He said he would always obey God.

Fighting for their beliefs

King Antiochus was very angry. He sent his soldiers to kill the rebels. Mattathias, his five sons, and some Jewish followers fled to the hills. Other families joined them.

Mattathias decided that the only way the Jews could survive against the King's soldiers was to fight back. The group lived together in the caves of Judea and gave one another strength. They began to teach themselves ways of fighting back. They asked God for help in defeating their enemy.

Mattathias died and his son Judah took his place as leader. Judah and all his followers became known as the Maccabees. Maccabee means hammer. The Maccabees fought on against the armies of Antiochus. They fought for three long years. They believed that God would help them to survive.

Victory at last!

Over the years, the soldiers of King Antiochus lost battle after battle. Finally, they realized they could never defeat the strong faith and courage of the Jews. They stopped fighting. At last, the Jews were free!

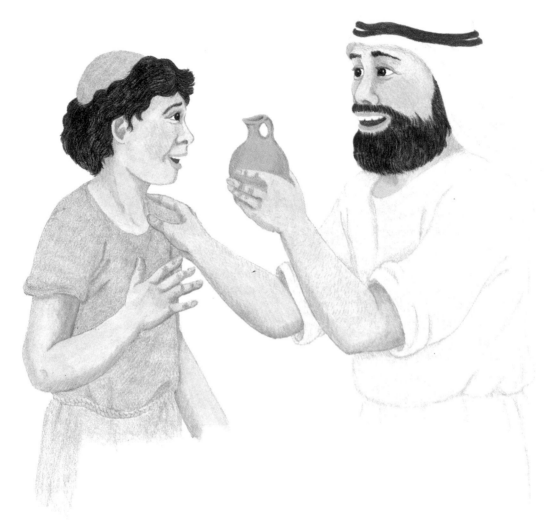

Cleaning the Temple

The Jews had built a beautiful Temple in Jerusalem, the capital of Judea. Before King Antiochus had forbidden them to follow their religion, they had worshipped God in this Temple. Then Antiochus' soldiers took over the Temple and put up an altar to their own gods. When the Maccabees won their final battle, they cleaned the Temple. They tore down the Greek altar. They built a new one. They planted trees in the courtyard.

The Jews were happy to see that the menorah was still in the Temple. The menorah was a tall, golden candlestick with seven branches. Each branch had a cup. The cups were always supposed to be filled with pure olive oil. The wicks in the oil were to be burning at all times. Since the menorah in the Temple had not been lit since Antiochus' soldiers had taken over, the Jews had no holy oil with which to light the menorah.

The miracle of the oil

Suddenly, while cleaning the Temple, someone found a small jar of olive oil. The oil was put in the menorah and lit. There was only enough oil to last for one day. The next day, everyone was astonished to find that the oil was still burning brightly. In fact, the oil kept burning for eight days!

Ever since then, the Hanukkah celebration has lasted for eight days to honor this miracle. Hanukkah is the Hebrew word for "dedicated." The holiday reminds Jews of the time long ago when Judah and the Maccabees dedicated the Temple to God again. The Hanukkah menorah now has eight branches and eight candles — one for each night of the celebration, with one added branch for the *shamash*, the ninth candle.

Today, during the eight days of Hanukkah, Jews remember how God helped them to win their freedom. They remember the strong faith of the Maccabees. They remember the special miracle of the oil that brought light to the first Hanukkah celebration. They pray that people everywhere will be allowed to live in peace and be free to follow their own beliefs.

When does Hanukkah come?

Hanukkah is usually in December. The month of December belongs to the Gregorian calendar. Many people around the world use the Gregorian calendar. It is a solar calendar. That means it is based on the movement of the sun. When the earth travels once around the sun, this is one solar year. There are 365 days in the solar year. According to the Gregorian calendar, the seasons begin and end close to the same date every year.

A lunar calendar

Hanukkah does not fall on the same date each year on the Gregorian calendar, because the day on which Hanukkah falls is determined by the Jewish calendar. The Jewish calendar is different from the Gregorian calendar. It is a lunar calendar. This means that it is based on the movement of the moon.

The moon circles the earth every 29½ days. The Jewish calendar is based on these lunar cycles. Each cycle of the moon is one month on the Jewish calendar. Since we cannot switch months in the middle of the day, certain months have twenty-nine days while others have thirty days. Thus, a Jewish month has either twenty-nine or thirty days.

A seasonal problem

The Jewish calendar year is eleven days shorter than a solar year. There are 354 days in the Jewish calendar year. A lunar calendar is not arranged according to the seasons. However, there are many holidays that celebrate seasons, such as the spring tree-planting festival. In order for the lunar calendar holidays to match the seasons they celebrate, a leap year occurs every two or three years. A Jewish leap year adds on a whole month. This leap-year month adds the lost days back to the year. It helps the Jewish calendar stay in line with the seasons and the solar year.

10

The twenty-fifth day of Kislev

There are twelve months in the Jewish calendar year. The months are: Tishri, Heshvan, Kislev, Tevet, Shevat, Adar, Nisan, Iyar, Sivan, Tammuz, Av, and Elul. Hanukkah celebrations begin on the twenty-fifth of Kislev and continue for eight days. The first day of Kislev occurs in November or December.

The changing dates of Hanukkah

Look at this year's calendar. Is Hanukkah marked on it? On what day does it begin? Find the date of Hanukkah on last year's calendar. Did Hanukkah begin on the same date last year as it does this year? How much difference is there between last year's date and the date of Hanukkah on this year's calendar?

Make your own calendar

Invent a calendar. You will have to decide many things about your calendar. How many months will there be in your calendar year? How many days will there be in each month? Decide if you will have weeks in your year. Decide how many days there will be in each week. Invent names for the months, weeks, and days. Mark special days, such as your birthday, on your calendar. Is your year longer or shorter than a year on the Jewish calendar? What is your age according to your new calendar?

A celebration of peace

People are different from one another. They have different religions. They celebrate holidays in different ways. They wear different clothes and speak different languages.

Do you look just like your friends? Of course not! Do you always agree with your parents? Of course not! You are a special person. You are unique. No one is just like you!

It's fun to be different. Can you imagine what a dull place the world would be if we all looked the same or believed the same things? Imagine a world without different colors, noises, animals, feelings, or hopes. Differences make the world an exciting place.

Hurray for differences!

Sometimes, people who do not share the same beliefs have trouble getting along with one another. King Antiochus thought everyone should live in a certain way and believe what he believed. Today, many people of different beliefs and backgrounds have learned to live peacefully together. They have learned to share the things they have in common and enjoy their differences. This is something to celebrate!

Shout and jump for peace.
Let's all join hands and sing.
Together we can celebrate
The differences we bring!

A joyful time

Families spend time together on one or all of the eight evenings of Hanukkah. They sing songs, eat, and play games. They tell stories of the Maccabees and remember their own family histories.

Lighting the menorah is the most important part of the Hanukkah celebrations. Families gather around it just after dark. In some Jewish homes, each member of the family lights his or her own menorah at Hanukkah. In other homes, family members take turns lighting one menorah. The light of the menorah in the darkness reminds Jews of the faith and courage of the Maccabees during dark and lonely times.

14

The shamash

The menorah is a candelabrum with eight branches and an added branch for the *shamash*, the ninth candle. Shamash means servant. The shamash is lit with a match, and is used to light the eight Hanukkah candles. The candles are lit to remind Jews of the miracle of Hanukkah. They cannot be used for work, and so they cannot be used to light one another. This is why the shamash is used.

After the shamash lights the other candles, it is placed in the ninth candleholder of the menorah. This ninth position is sometimes on a different level from that of the other candleholders.

Thanking God

After the shamash is lit, but before the other candles are lit, the family recites a blessing together. They thank God for his laws and for the Hanukkah miracle. On the first night of Hanukkah, a third prayer is added. This prayer thanks God for giving life and allowing everyone to celebrate this special time of year.

Lighting the candles one by one

On the first night of Hanukkah, only one candle is lit by the shamash. This candle is placed in the holder on the far right as you face the menorah. On the second night, two new candles are lit by the shamash. The first candle is placed on the far right and the second candle is placed to the left of this candle. The second candle is lit first. Then the first candle is lit. Each night, for six more nights, one more candle is added to the menorah. The candles are put in from right to left. But they are lit from left to right. In this way, each candle position has a night to hold the candle that is first lit.

Sharing the joy

Each night after the menorah is lit, it is placed on the windowsill so everyone on the street can see its light. In this way, the joy of Hanukkah is shared by all!

See them glow

Light the candles! See them glow
Proudly standing in a row.

Flickering, fluttering, never still,
Together on the windowsill.

Light the candles one by one
As God to darkness brings the sun.

A flame of hope, a flame of love,
The candles tell of God above.

Light the candles, light our hearts.
This is where our courage starts.

See them shine their little light,
A brave, bright signal in the night.

They speak to us of present and past.
They promise future peace to last.

Light the candles! See them glow
Proudly standing in a row.

Make a clay menorah

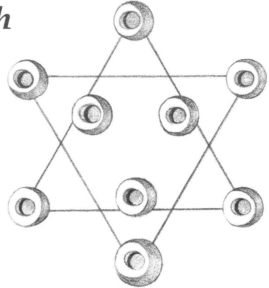

There are many ways to make a menorah for your Hanukkah celebration. Buy some clay from a craft store. Divide and roll the clay into nine balls, leaving a small amount aside. Push the end of a pencil into the middle of each ball. This will make holes into which you can insert small Hanukkah candles. Arrange the nine clay containers and their candles in a row, a circle, or in the shape of the Star of David. The Star of David is a six-pointed star. It is the symbol of Judaism and Israel.

Add the leftover clay to the bottom of the ninth container so that its candle stands higher than the other eight candles. This holder is for the shamash.

A simple thimble craft

Make a menorah with metal thimbles! Collect nine metal thimbles. Find a large piece of styrofoam. Cover the styrofoam in foil. Now, push the end of a pencil through the foil and into the styrofoam. Push and twist until there is a thimble-sized hole. Make seven more holes in this manner. Then insert the thimbles, open-side up, into the holes. Put one thin candle into each thimble.

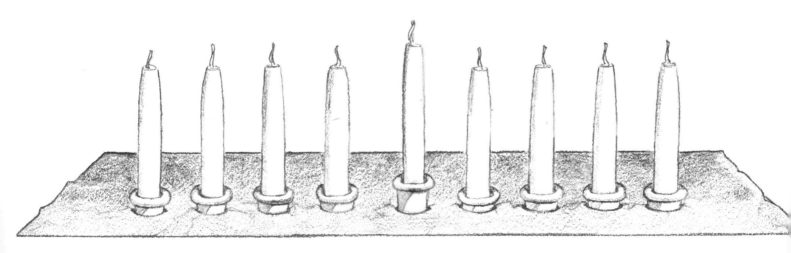

18

Make a ninth hole, but do not make it as deep as the others. The ninth thimble and its candle or shamash will stand higher.

The candles may not be steady in the thimbles. Have an adult or an older friend help you to secure them by lighting a match and heating the wax on the bottom of each one. The melted wax will harden and secure the candles when they are pressed into the thimbles.

Lit without a match!

Make a paper menorah to hang in your window. On a piece of construction paper, draw the outline of a menorah. Draw candles in its holders. Carefully cut out the menorah. Tape colorful tissue paper over the cut-out hole.

Hang your construction-paper menorah in the window. Make sure the side with the tape faces the window and the other side faces you! The light of the sun or the moon shining behind your menorah will make it appear to glow with its own candlelight!

Festivals of light

Hanukkah is a festival of light. There are many other celebrations that light up the darkness. All over the world during festivals of every kind, firecrackers streak colors across the sky. Candles, colored lights, sparklers, and bonfires glow!

The festival of Diwali is a Hindu celebration. Many Indians light small clay lamps called *dipas* during this festival. They place them on windowsills and roofs. Young girls float them down rivers. If the dipas reach the other side, the girls believe they will have good luck in the new year.

In Japan, during the O-Bon festival, people light bonfires and lanterns to guide the spirits of family and friends down to earth for the festival days!

In Sweden, December 13 is Saint Lucia Day. Saint Lucia lived hundreds of years ago. She taught people about Jesus. Young girls dress up as Saint Lucia on December 13. They wear a crown of six candles! Star boys accompany Saint Lucia. They carry cutouts of stars on long wands.

At Christmas time around the world, people decorate their homes and Christmas trees with colored lights or candles. The lights stand for peace, hope, and love.

21

What it means to me

Deborah sat at the living-room table. She was bent over a piece of paper that was covered with sentences — all of them scratched out. She sighed and rested her head on her hands.

"I'll never finish this assignment," she said aloud to herself. " 'The Light of Hanukkah and What it Means to Me.' What a topic for an essay! Hanukkah is just another holiday. That's the problem."

Deborah sighed again. She watched the flickering flames on the menorah. "The Light of Hanukkah," she said aloud again. She tapped her pencil on the table. "The problem is that Hannukah is all about an old story. The Maccabees fought battles and won. Then they lit the menorah in the Temple and it shone for eight days. Those flames meant something to the Maccabees, but how can they mean anything to me? I wasn't even born yet!"

Deborah scratched her head. She closed one eye and looked at her paper.

She twisted a lock of hair around her finger and looked at the candle flames. She thought and thought. "I just can't do this assignment. It's due tomorrow, and I haven't written a word."

Suddenly, all the lights in the apartment went out. Only the small area lit by the menorah was visible. "Oh no!" moaned Deborah. "A blackout! What a night for this to happen. How can I do my assignment in the dark?"

Then Deborah had an idea. If she sat near the menorah, she could use its light. She stood up and took her paper and pencil to an armchair near the windowsill. The menorah had been placed there to shine its light out on the dark streets.

Then, just as quickly as Deborah had thought of her idea, she realized the plan was no good. "The light of the menorah cannot be used for work," she remembered. "What will I do? I must have this assignment finished by tomorrow!"

Deborah sat fidgeting on the edge of her armchair. She tapped her foot nervously. She was not thinking about what the light of Hanukkah meant to her. All she could do was worry about not being able to finish the assignment.

Then, slowly, Deborah began to relax in the darkened room. She stopped tapping her foot. She stopped fidgeting. The Hanukkah flames caught her eye. Their steady glow calmed her. She stopped worrying. She sat and watched the flames, feeling peaceful and suddenly happy.

The next morning, Deborah explained nervously to her teacher why she had no assignment to hand in. "I just finally fell asleep in the chair," she finished. Deborah waited anxiously for the teacher to assign her extra work or detentions.

Instead, the teacher smiled. "Deborah," he said. "You say the story of Hanukkah means nothing to you. You say you have not thought of any meaning that the candles of Hanukkah hold for you, but in the same breath you tell me that you felt peaceful sitting near the candles. You felt the candles melt away your problems." The teacher smiled at the look on Deborah's face. "Happy Hanukkah, Deborah," he said. "I think you have completed the assignment in your own way."

gelt

yarmulke

כ ג ה שׁ
nun gimmel hey shin

shamash

wick

candle

dreidel

menorah

challah

latkes

kugel

doughnuts

Torah

altar

tallis

rabbi

torch

Star of David

synagogue

Hanukkah words

Try to use all these words to write your own Hanukkah story.

Praying for peace

The Hanukkah candles are lit. They must burn for at least a half hour after sunset. The family members watch the flickering flames and remember the first Hanukkah. They try to imagine what it must have been like to be a member of the band of Maccabees. They thank God that the Maccabees were not destroyed. They think about their own families and friends and pray that there will be peace everywhere on earth.

A time for singing

The family members join hands and sing about God and Hanukkah. They sing songs such as "Rock of Ages" and "These Singing Lights."

Rock of Ages

Rock of Ages, let our song
Praise Thy saving power.
Thou amidst the raging foes
Wast our sheltering tower.

Furious they assailed us,
But Thine arm availed us,
And Thy word broke their sword
When our own strength failed us.
And Thy word broke their sword
When our own strength failed us.

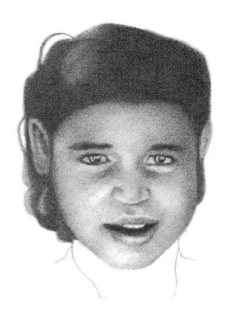

These Singing Lights

These singing lights
we light to remember
the miracle of our survival,
the miraculous victories and deliverances
out of wars and ashes
that sang in the eyes of our mothers and fathers
at these very days of the year
just as the priests used to sing in the Temple
in ancient days.

Through the full eight days of Hanukkah,
these singing lights are deeply felt
for their light is not to see by,
not to use in the ordinary world,
but to behold and feel
like a memory deep within —
like a chord of praise
struck by light
inspiring us to sing
in the name of what's held holy
that we have been delivered to this day
in the miracle of our lives.

Foods for a feast

Hanukkah is a time for special foods. Years ago, in Israel, children used to go from home to home during the first days of Hanukkah. They collected food for family dinners. They sang:

Give us heaps of flour —
Your lives will never go sour!
Give us jars of oil —
The Lord your foes will foil!

Some children recited verses from the Holy Book. They chose the verses which mentioned food.

The Feast of Dedication

On the last day of Hanukkah, it was a custom for the children to go from home to home with their teachers. Sometimes, they carried burning candles. They sang songs and chanted, "Buy us a little food." Some students sang:

"Prepare the meals and the great celebration,
    When all will share in the Feast of Dedication."

Did you remember that the word "hanukkah" means dedication?
The Feast of Dedication was the great Hanukkah feast.

The children and teachers collected onions, vegetables, fruit, chicken or other fowl, and flour. Then the children prepared three meals. One meal was for the poor, one was for the teachers, and one was for themselves!

Sharing a meal

Today, eating together is still a big part of Hanukkah celebrations. People like to be together on holidays. Families, children, teachers, friends, and neighbors meet for a special Hanukkah dinner. Hospitals and retirement homes have festive meals. Friends bring together people who have had arguments. They sit and eat together, and usually the disagreements disappear. Hanukkah is a time for friendship and sharing.

Special Hanukkah foods

There is a variety of special Hanukkah foods eaten by Jews around the world. Many of these foods are cooked with oil. At Hanukkah, people celebrate the miracle of the oil by cooking with oil! *Latkes* are a favorite dish. They are pancakes made from grated potatoes. Some families bake *pfanken*. Pfanken are cookies shaped like doughnuts. Turkish families fry puffy doughnuts in oil. Eastern European Jews eat a kind of pudding called *kugel*. They also enjoy a roast goose or duck on Hanukkah.

Let's get cooking!

Try some of these Hanukkah recipes with your family or older friends. Be sure you make enough food, though. People always seem to be hungry during the week of Hanukkah!

Latkes

6 large potatoes
3 eggs
1 small onion, chopped
60 mL (¼ cup) flour
5 mL (1 teaspoon) salt
1 mL (¼ teaspoon) pepper
15 mL (1 tablespoon) oil
10 mL (2 teaspoons) baking
  powder
oil for frying

1. Wash potatoes. Peel and grate them. Squeeze out as much liquid as possible.
2. In a small bowl, beat eggs.
3. Mix together potatoes, eggs, onion, flour, salt, pepper, 15 mL (1 tablespoon) oil, and baking powder.
4. Heat remaining oil in frying pan. When oil is hot, drop some of the potato mixture into pan. (Use one tablespoon of the mixture for each latke.) Stand back — the oil can splatter.

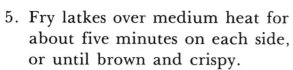

5. Fry latkes over medium heat for about five minutes on each side, or until brown and crispy.
6. Remove latkes from pan and dry on paper towels. Fry remaining mixture.

This recipe serves six to eight people. Serve the latkes hot with applesauce.

Plain Noodle Kugel

200 g (8 ounces) egg noodles
5 eggs
salt
pepper
90 mL (6 tablespoons) oil
125 mL (½ cup) raisins

1. Cook noodles (using instructions on noodle package).
2. Beat eggs in mixing bowl.
3. Mix cooked noodles with eggs, dash of salt and pepper, raisins, and 45 mL (3 tablespoons) of oil.
4. Use the remaining oil to grease a baking dish.
5. Preheat oven to 190°C (375°F). Heat dish in oven.
6. When oil in dish is hot, pour noodle mixture into dish and place in oven.
7. Bake for one hour.

Menorah Salad

lettuce leaves
9 pineapple rings
9 small bananas
lemon juice
9 maraschino cherries
cottage cheese or sour cream

1. Separate lettuce leaves and arrange in a row on a large platter.
2. Place pineapple rings in a row along the leaves to form the base of the menorah.
3. Cut off one end of each banana, leaving the end flat.
4. Dip the bananas in lemon juice. (This keeps them from turning brown.)
5. Stand each banana on its flat end in a pineapple ring.
6. Scoop out a small portion of the rounded end of each banana. Set a cherry in each of the scooped-out ends. The bananas are like the candles in the menorah. The cherries are like the flames on the candles.
7. Serve the menorah salad with cottage cheese or sour cream.

Serves nine.

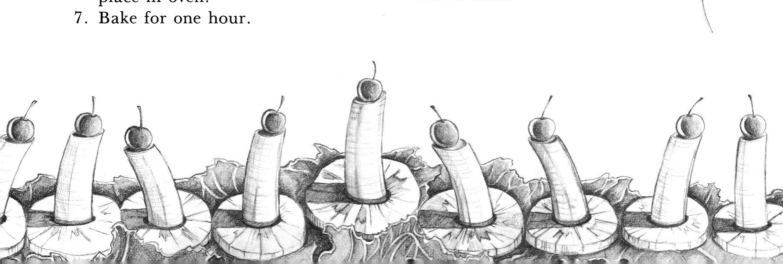

Happy endings

The Hanukkah meal is over and the family is together. What a good time to tell stories! Storytelling is an old Hanukkah tradition. The children sit near the storyteller so they can hear every word. They listen with excitement to stories of the Maccabean battles. They sigh with relief at the happy ending, even though they have heard these stories many times before. The stories have been told to children for hundreds of years at Hanukkah time.

New tales, new games

Hanukkah is a time for new stories, too. These new tales are about learning to live together and sharing different beliefs and ways of life.

After the storytelling, there is still time to play games before bedtime. Card games are popular. Make a deck of ordinary cards into a special Maccabean deck. Put sticky labels on the cards and draw Hanukkah symbols on the labels. Make up ways to change your favorite card games into Hanukkah card games.

Board games can be turned into Hanukkah games, too. Play Scrabble and add the rule that any word that is related to Hanukkah gives you ten extra points! Play chess or checkers. Call one set of pieces the Maccabees and the other set of pieces the soldiers of Antiochus. Which side will win this battle?

That special number forty-four

Number games that add up to forty-four are called *kattoves*. They are popular Hanukkah games. The number forty-four is a special number because it is the total number of candles lit during the eight days of Hanukkah. Count them: one candle is lit the first evening, two candles are lit the second evening, then three, four, five, six, seven, and finally, eight candles are lit on the final evening. These numbers add up to thirty-six. The shamash is lit every night for eight nights. Add another eight to thirty-six. This adds up to forty-four.

Try this game. Mark sixteen squares on a piece of paper, with four rows of four squares. Put the following numbers in the boxes so that each row of four numbers — across and down — adds up to forty-four:
3, 5, 8, 9, 10, 10, 10, 10, 11, 11, 12, 13, 14, 15, 15, 20

Answers:

11	11	10	12
10	15	9	10
13	3	20	8
10	15	5	14

Dreidel, dreidel, dreidel!

The most popular game to play at Hanukkah is dreidel. Dreidel has been played during Hanukkah for hundreds of years. A dreidel is like a top. It has four sides. Dreidels used to be made of lead or clay. Sometimes, children would carve their own dreidels out of wood. Today, many dreidels are made from plastic.

There is a different Hebrew letter for each of the four sides of the dreidel. Hebrew is a language that was first spoken by the ancient Jews. Now, it is the official language of Israel. It is the language of the Jewish religion.

A great miracle

The letters on the dreidel are 'n' or nun, 'g' or gimmel, 'h' or hey, and 'sh' or shin. Each letter begins a word in the Hebrew phrase, "Nes gadol hayah sham." This phrase means, "A great miracle happened there." Do you know what the miracle was? The miracle was the miracle of the oil and the miracle of the Maccabean victories. The miracle occurred in Israel. This is why the phrase says the miracle happened "there."

It happened here!

In Israel, the dreidel has a 'p' or peh instead of a 'sh'. 'P' stands for the word poh. Poh is a Hebrew word which means "here." In Israel, people say, "A great miracle happened here!"

HAYAH SHAM

A game of luck

Some people believe that the dreidel was invented during the time of the Maccabees. In the years after the first Hanukkah, the rabbis or teachers of the Jewish religion did not like the game because it is a game of luck. The rabbis believed that it was not proper to play games of luck. Later on, however, they decided that the dreidel game was a good way to fill the long, dark Hanukkah evenings. Besides which, the dreidel had a message of Hanukkah on its four sides. It reminded the players of the great miracle!

How to play

Any number of players can play dreidel. Each player must have an equal number of pennies, walnuts, raisins, or other markers. Each player puts one marker in the main pile. Then everyone takes a turn spinning the dreidel. The dreidel spins and finally falls on one side.

The letter that is on the top side will tell the player what to do.
Nun — Player does nothing.
Gimmel — Player gets all the markers in the main pile.
Hey — Player takes half the markers in the main pile.
Shin or **peh** — Player must set one marker in the main pile.

When the main pile is gone, the players must again put in equal numbers of markers. When a player has no more markers to put in, he or she is out of the game. The player that ends up with all the markers is the winner!

The secret of the dreidels

Some people believe that the game of dreidel had a very special beginning. Read this story and decide if you think this is the way the dreidel game might have become popular.

36

The great cover-up

Daniel and Seth were sitting in a circle with their friends. It was a warm summer day in Jerusalem, the capital of Judea. The courtyard was full of sunlight and the sound of the boys' voices.

"Can you explain this chapter to us, Daniel?" one of the boys said. Four young faces turned to look at Daniel.

Daniel smiled nervously. His brother, Seth, gave him an encouraging nod and a wink. The two brothers had spent extra time on their studies the night before. Together they had quietly recited chapters of the Torah.

"Yes, I can," said Daniel. He took a deep breath. Then he began his answer. Suddenly, one of the boys whispered, "Daniel, shhh. Soldiers."

Without turning their heads to look at the two large men coming toward them across the courtyard, several of the boys quickly reached into their pockets. They pulled out their dreidels. They began to spin the dreidels, loudly singing the Dreidel Song and cheering at the whirling tops.

Daniel carefully peeked out of the corner of his eye. He saw the soldiers draw nearer. Had the soldiers discovered their secret?

It was forbidden to study the Torah now that King Antiochus was the ruler of Judea. It was forbidden even to own a Torah. So all the boys worked hard to memorize parts of the holy works. They carried the words in their heads and hearts. The boys met openly every day in the courtyard to study the meaning of God's words.

If the soldiers had guessed that the boys were studying the holy laws in the sunny courtyard, they would have punished them severely. The boys kept playing as the soldiers stood nearby, watching them.

"Oh, dreidel, dreidel, dreidel! I made it out of clay," they sang. Their hearts were pounding, so the boys sang even louder. Finally, the soldiers turned to leave. Daniel heard one of them say, "Stupid boys. They've got nothing better to do than to sit and play silly games."

Daniel laughed. The secret of the dreidels was still safe! As the other boys listened closely, Daniel smiled and again began to explain the chapter. The dreidels lay still on the ground but within reach — in case the soldiers returned.

Oh, dreidel I will play!

Here is a song to help you remember the rules of the dreidel game.

A Dreidel Song

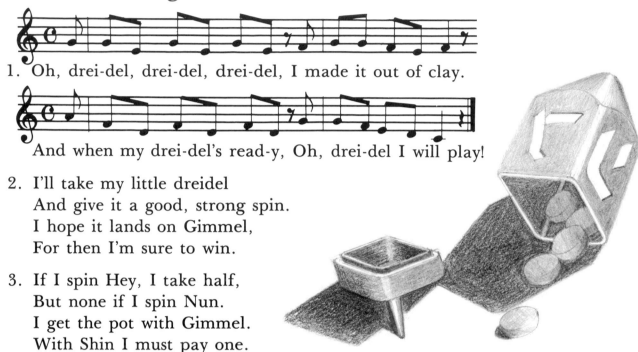

1. Oh, drei-del, drei-del, drei-del, I made it out of clay.

And when my drei-del's read-y, Oh, drei-del I will play!

2. I'll take my little dreidel
   And give it a good, strong spin.
   I hope it lands on Gimmel,
   For then I'm sure to win.

3. If I spin Hey, I take half,
   But none if I spin Nun.
   I get the pot with Gimmel.
   With Shin I must pay one.

Make your own dreidels

Make a simple dreidel out of construction paper or cardboard. Look at the pattern below. It looks like a hopscotch game! Copy this pattern onto your paper or cardboard. Cut the pattern out in one piece. Cut out the two small holes that you have marked on the pattern.

The Hebrew symbols for the four dreidel letters are:
nun — **נ** ,   gimmel — **ג** ,   hey — **ה** ,   and shin — **ש** .
Draw these letters on the four sides that do not have holes. Now fold the paper or cardboard along the inside lines to form a box. Tape the folds.

Poke a pencil through the holes. If the holes are too big, the pencil will fall out of the box. Cover the holes with tape and push the pencil through the tape. Now the box will remain on the pencil. Spin the pencil. Your homemade dreidel is finished!

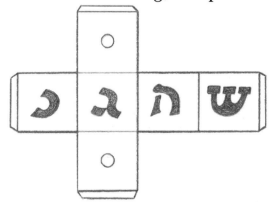

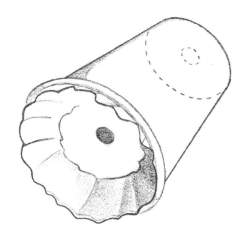

A paper-cup dreidel

Here is another easy way to make a dreidel. Find a small, white paper cup. Use a sharp pencil to poke a hole in the center of the bottom of the cup. Draw the four Hebrew letters along the sides of the cup.

Place the open rim of the cup on a piece of heavy paper. Trace the rim. Draw another circle around this first circle. Draw the second circle about 2.5 cm (1 inch) larger than the smaller circle. Now, cut out this large circle and a small hole in the center of the small circle. Fold along the small circle.

Put drops of glue along the inside of the cup, close to the rim. Insert the folded circle into the cup so that the folds will stick to the glue and the circle will form a bottom for the cup. Push a long pencil through the two holes. Spin your paper-cup dreidel!

Old and new

Invent your own dreidels. Use plastic containers, pieces of egg carton, styrofoam, table-tennis balls, or small boxes. Decorate the dreidels with materials from your home, such as sequins, buttons, paper clips, or string. Have a contest with your friends to see who can make the most unusual dreidel. Have a dreidel show. Make up special songs to sing for each dreidel you spin!

Sharing at Hanukkah

Hanukkah is a time for giving and sharing. People spend time together sharing the joy of the Hanukkah miracles. Spending time with other people is one of the best Hanukkah gifts you can give!

Hanukkah gelt

Hundreds of years ago at Hanukkah, parents thanked their children's teachers for working so hard teaching their children. They gave them money. This gift of money was called *gelt*. Gelt is the Yiddish word for "money." Yiddish is a language that uses Hebrew letters. It is spoken mostly by Jews in Europe and Israel.

Some people baked the teachers special cakes with Hanukkah coins inside! In Turkey, people baked platefuls of latkes and carried them from home to home. Generous people were given three of these latkes if they donated Hanukkah gelt. The gelt was collected and given to the poor.

Old coins, new coins

Some people believe that the tradition of giving gelt at Hanukkah began soon after the Maccabees won their last battle. The coins used in Judea had the profile of King Antiochus stamped on them. When the soldiers of Antiochus fled and the Jews began to rule Judea again, the Jews threw away all the Antiochus coins. They made new coins with the profile of Judah Maccabee on them. These coins reminded the Jews that they were free again! Perhaps these new coins began the tradition of giving gelt at Hanukkah.

Good enough to eat

Today at Hanukkah, many Jewish children are given gelt by their parents and relatives. Some families have changed this tradition. Instead of gelt, they give candy coins or chocolate coins wrapped in gold foil. Parents may hide these edible coins throughout the home. The children must go on a treasure hunt to find the shiny treats.

Gift-giving

In North America, many people give wrapped gifts to their children. Some children are given a gift on one of the eight evenings of Hanukkah. Others are given a small gift on each night of the holiday. Giving gifts is a small but fun part of the Hanukkah celebrations!

Homemade Hanukkah gifts

Why not surprise your friends and family members with homemade Hanukkah gifts? One very special gift that you can give is a gift of time. Cut out and decorate strips of cardboard. On one side of the cardboard, write: "I want to share some time with you." On the other side, write the date and the amount of time you would like to share. You can arrange the activities later. Perhaps you might bake cookies with your mother, read a story with your grandfather, or go for a walk with a younger sister or brother.

Hanukkah puppets

Make puppets for your friends. On a piece of cardboard, draw characters such as Judah and Mattathias, other members of the Maccabee band, or King Antiochus. Cut out the characters. Tape a popsicle stick, drinking straw or pencil to the back of each character so that the bottom half of the stick, straw, or pencil can be held in your hand.

Make a Shadow Box

Cut the flaps off a cardboard carton. Cut a square out of the bottom of the box so that when it is set on its side, the box will look like a TV set. Tape tracing paper or tissue paper across this opening. This will make a screen. Invite your friends to hold their stick puppets behind the Shadow Box. Place a lamp or hold a flashlight behind the box so that a bright light shines on the puppets and the screen. The audience looking at the front of the box will see the shadows of the puppets moving across the screen. With your friends, put on a Hanukkah puppet show for everyone to enjoy!

I promise to help

Another special gift is a promise to help. Make a card by folding a blank piece of plain paper or construction paper in half. Color the card or cut out and paste Hanukkah symbols on it. Some Hanukkah symbols are a menorah, a candle, a dreidel, and a Star of David.

Inside the card, print the words: "I promise to . . ." Complete the sentence by filling in an activity you could do to help the person who gets this gift. It might be a promise to wash the dishes, to help in the garden, to write a letter, or to help with homework. Use your imagination to come up with ideas that your friends and family will enjoy.

The useful potato

Make Hanukkah cards using one of the favorite Hanukkah meal ingredients — the potato! Cut a potato in half. Draw a simple Hanukkah symbol on the potato half. You may want to draw the four dreidel letters, a dreidel, or the Star of David. Have an older friend or an adult help you use a knife to carve around the symbol so that the symbol becomes raised.

Fold a piece of white paper in half. This will be the card. Press the potato symbol onto an ink pad or a shallow dish of paint. Try to let the ink or paint collect only on the raised symbol and not on the rest of the potato. Press the symbol onto the card several times, making any design you wish. When the card is dry, write a Hanukkah message inside.

You can try cutting different parts of one symbol into several potato halves. Use one potato half for a candle and another for a flame. Dip them in different colors of paint and decorate your cards with them.

A zany Hanukkah

How many things can you count in this picture that are making this a zany Hanukkah for Rob and Laura?

44

Ways of celebrating

Jews live in many countries. At Hanukkah around the world, they share many of the same traditions. They light the Hanukkah candles. They visit with family and friends. In some countries, Jews have added their own customs to the traditional Hanukkah celebrations.

Did you know that in Syria, Jewish children receive special gifts at Hanukkah? One gift may be a candle in the shape of a hand! In Syria and other Middle Eastern countries, the hand is a sign of protection.

Did you know that in many countries during Hanukkah week, Hebrew schools are open for half-days only? The teachers tell the story of the miracle of the oil. The children play games and put on Hanukkah plays. There are special assemblies and classroom parties.

Did you know that in Israel, Hanukkah is a national holiday? The schools close and businesses shut down. The days are filled with parties, picnics, and sporting events. People put menorahs on their windowsills and huge electric menorahs are placed on top of tall buildings.

Did you know that in Israel, the most exciting part of the Hanukkah celebrations is the torch relay? The relay begins in Modin, the town where Mattathias lived. It is very near Jerusalem. A large bonfire is lit in the town. The first runner dips the torch into the flames and then runs toward Jerusalem. Other runners are waiting along the road. The torch is passed from runner to runner. The thousands of spectators lining the road cheer and clap as the Torch of Freedom is carried past.

The last runner stops at the Western Wall in Jerusalem. The Western Wall is the only remaining part of the ancient Temple. There is a giant menorah on the Western Wall. The runner hands the torch to the chief rabbi, and the rabbi uses the torch to kindle the first light of the menorah.

Did you ever think of having a relay in your community? Runners can carry a "torch" made of cardboard or construction paper, or they can carry a flag with Jewish symbols. Have the relay route pass different Jewish institutions in your neighborhood. Perhaps the relay can finish at a synagogue or Jewish community center where a large outdoor menorah is displayed.

Did you know that in some Middle Eastern countries, menorahs used to be lit in the morning? The menorahs were often very simple. They were eggshell halves filled with olive oil. Children made puppets and drew pictures of Antiochus. In the evenings, they carried the puppets and drawings from home to home and collected Hanukkah gelt. At the end of the evening, the children put the puppets and drawings on a bonfire. They shouted, "Antiochus! Antiochus!" as the fire burned.

Did you know that in Venice, Italy, some Jews spend the evening in boats? In Venice, canals crisscross the city. People travel along the canals in gondolas, which are long, narrow boats. During the Hanukkah evenings, the lights from the menorahs in the windowsills of Jewish homes reflect on the water in the canal. Some Jews travel in gondolas from one candlelit window to another. They shout out Hanukkah greetings and sing cheerful Hanukkah songs.

Preparing for a Hanukkah party!

Celebrate Hanukkah this year by having a classroom party. Decorate the room with handmade decorations. Favorite Hanukkah colors are royal blue and white. These are the colors on the flag of Israel. Use these colors in your decorations.

Cut out pieces of cardboard in the shapes of dreidels, gelt, or Stars of David. Use felt markers, crayons, or pastels to add color to the decorations. Glue on tissue-paper balls, sparkles, stars, or ribbons. Use a needle to string colored popcorn onto a long thread. Hang the decorations around the classroom.

Make paper chains

First, cut a strip of construction paper. Glue the ends of the strip together, making a ring. Now cut another strip of paper. Put one end of the strip through the first paper ring. Glue the ends of the strip together. The two rings will be connected. Continue making strips and adding them to the chain. Dangle or drape the chain across the room.

49

Hanukkah games

Try to plan party activities that have a Hanukkah theme.

Don't say "eight!"

Play Counting up to Hanukkah. How many days of Hanukkah are there? Eight! Eight will play a special part in this game.

Have the players sit in a circle. The first player begins by saying, "One." The player on his or her right says, "Two." The counting continues around the circle, but no player may say the number eight, a number with an eight in it (such as eighteen or twenty-eight), or a multiple of eight (such as sixteen or twenty-four). Instead of saying these numbers, the player must say, "Hanukkah." Each time the word "Hanukkah" is said, the counting must change direction around the circle. If a player makes a mistake, the counting begins again at the number one. If a player makes two mistakes, he or she must leave the circle. Play this game slowly at first. As you improve, speed up the pace!

Oops

Oops is a Hanukkah clapping game. A leader is picked and gives each player a word that has something to do with Hanukkah. Such words may include dreidel, latke, Mattathias, Star of David, gelt, Maccabee, menorah, Judah, or candle. The players sit in a circle around the leader. The leader tells a story about Hanukkah, using the words he or she has given out to the players.

When the leader uses the word "Hanukkah," all the players clap their hands twice. When a word that has been given to a player is said, that player must clap once.

If a player does not clap when his or her word or the word "Hanukkah" is said, the player is given the first letter of the word "Oops." The second time the player makes a mistake, he or she is given the second letter of the word "Oops." When a player has been given all the letters in the word "Oops," the player is out of the game. The leader may have to tell a long story and use the special Hanukkah words many times before there is a winner in this game!

Making the past the present

Act out the story of the Maccabees. The players can choose roles. One player can be the narrator and tell the story while the others silently act out the narrator's words.

Afterwards, the characters can interview one another. What would you like to know if you could speak to these important people of the past? Would you ask Judah how he felt when his father, Mattathias, died? Would you ask one of the members of the Maccabee band what he or she did to celebrate the first Hanukkah? Would you ask King Antiochus how he felt when the Jews defeated his soldiers? Use your imagination in asking questions and answering them!

52

Be My Shadow

The flames from the Hanukkah candles throw dancing shadows in the dark room. See if your classmates can be Hanukkah shadows when they play the game Be My Shadow.

Two players sit in two chairs placed back to back. The players must not see each other. Each player is given a bag or a box filled with the same objects. These objects may include a piece of paper, a book, a pair of socks, or a rope.

The first player moves his or her body to a certain position and then instructs the other player, her "shadow," to do the same. For example: "Cross your left leg over your right leg, and close your right eye." The first player then uses the objects. She may wear one sock over her left shoe, tie the rope around her waist, place the book open at page ten on her lap, and tear a triangle from the paper and place it on her head. She must instruct the other player to do all these things.

When the players are finished, the other guests must judge whether the shadow has done a good job of following the instructions. Then two other players try to play Be My Shadow.

The last night of Hanukkah

The sun is quickly setting.
It's time for us to go.
We pull on heavy boots
And set off through the snow.

Frost nips at our noses.
Our breath looks like a cloud.
I hold my brother's hand
As we sing a song aloud.

We see our Grandpa's house,
There's his smiling face!
He's waving through the window.
To the door, we quickly race.

Beside the brass menorah
With its nine candles lit,
Grandpa serves us cookies
As we in armchairs sit.

He tells familiar stories
Of days when he was young.
He recites his favorite poems
And sings songs that were sung.

We listen to him with wonder.
We love this Hanukkah night
That we always spend with Grandpa
In the golden candlelight.

Soon the evening's over.
It is time for us to leave.
As we put on coats and mittens,
Grandpa reaches up his sleeve.

He pulls out golden coins.
"Here's gelt for both of you!"
He says this with a smile.
"And happy Hanukkah, too!"

It's always a surprise
Though it happens every year!
We kiss our dear old Grandpa
Who grins from ear to ear.

Now it's really time to go.
Our favorite day is done.
We leave our very best friend,
And call, "Thanks for all the fun!"

Index

altar, 8, 25
Antiochus, 6-8, 13, 37, 41, 47, 51
calendars, 10-11
Celebrate with us, 5
challah, 24
Christmas, 21
crafts:
    make your own calendar, 11
    menorahs, 18-19
    dreidels, 38-39
    Hanukkah puppets, 42
    Shadow box, 42
    "I promise to help" card, 43
    party decorations, 48-49
    potato stamps, 43
Diwali, 20
dreidels, 5, 24, 34-35, 36, 37-39, 43, 50
Dreidel Song, A, 38
Feast of Dedication, 28, 29
flag of Israel, 48
games:
    cards, 33
    scrabble, 33
    kattoves, 33
    dreidel, 34-35
    Don't say "eight", 50
    Oops, 50-51
    past and present, 51
    Be My Shadow, 53
gelt, 5, 40-41, 47, 50, 54
gifts, 41-43
gondolas, 47
great cover-up, The, 36-37
Hebrew, 9, 34
Hebrew schools, 46
Hindu, 20
Holy oil, 8
Israel, 6, 18, 34, 46
Japan, 21
Jerusalem, 8, 37, 46
Jewish calendar, 10-11
Jordan, 6
Judaism, 6-7
Judea, 6-8, 37, 41
kattoves, 33

King Antiochus, 6-8, 13, 37, 41, 47, 51
Kislev, 5, 11
kugel, 24, 30, 31
Last night of Hanukkah,The, 54
latkes, 5, 24, 30-31, 50
Maccabees, 5, 7-9, 14-15, 22, 26, 34-35,
    41, 50, 51
menorah, 5, 8-9, 14-15, 18-19, 24, 43,
    46-47, 50, 54
Middle East, 47
miracle of the oil, 8-9, 30, 34-35
miracle of the oil, The 8-9
Modin, 7, 46
O-Bon festival, 21
Palestine, 6
party, 48
pfanken, 30
rabbi, 25, 35, 46
recipes:
    latkes, 30-31
    plain noodle kugel, 31
    menorah salad, 31
Rock of Ages, 5, 26
Saint Lucia Day, 21
See them glow, 17
shamash, 9, 15
songs:
    A Dreidel Song, 38
    Rock of Ages, 26
    These Singing Lights, 26, 27
Star of David, 18, 25, 43, 48, 50
storytelling, 32-33
Sweden, 21
synagogue, 25
Syria, 46
tallis, 25
These Singing Lights, 26-27
Torah, 7, 25, 28, 37
Torch of Freedom, 46
torch relay, 46
Venice, Italy, 47
Western Wall, 46
What it means to me, 22-23
yarmulke, 24
Yiddish, 40

101112131415 LB Printed in the U.S.A. 98765432